LEAR━━━━**BOOK**

AUTHOR: Camilla de la Bédoyère
EDITORIAL: John Cattermole, Sarah Goulding, Julia Rolf, Polly Prior
DESIGN: Jennifer Bishop
ILLUSTRATORS: Bridget Dowty and Sarah Wimperis of Graham-Cameron Illustration
PRODUCTION: Chris Herbert, Claire Walker

PROJECT EDITOR: Catherine Taylor
PUBLISHER AND CREATIVE DIRECTOR: Nick Wells
Special thanks to John Coe.

FLAME TREE PUBLISHING
Crabtree Hall, Crabtree Lane
Fulham, Lond
United Kingd
www.flametr

This edition first published 2013

17 16 15 14 13
10 9 8 7 6 5 4 3 2 1

© 2013 Flame Tree Publishing Ltd

A CIP record for this book is available from the British Library upon request.

ISBN 978 0 85775 632 9

Printed in China

Foreword

Sometimes when I am crossing the playground on my way to visit a primary school I pass young children playing at schools. There is always a stern authoritarian little teacher at the front laying down the law to the unruly group of children in the pretend class. This puzzles me a little because the school I am visiting is very far from being like the children's play. Where do they get this Victorian view of what school is like? Perhaps it's handed down from generation to generation through the genes. Certainly they don't get it from their primary school. Teachers today are more often found alongside their pupils, who are learning by actually doing things for themselves, rather than merely listening and obeying instructions.

Busy children, interested and involved in their classroom reflect what we know about how they learn. Of course they learn from teachers but most of all they learn from their experience of life and their life is spent both in and out of school. Indeed, if we compare the impact upon children of even the finest schools and teachers, we find that three or four times as great an impact is made by the reality of children's lives outside the school. That reality has the parent at the all important centre. No adult can have so much impact, for good or ill, as the young child's mother or father.

This book, and others in the series, are founded on the sure belief that the great majority of parents want to help their children grow and learn and that teachers are keen to support them. The days when parents were kept at arm's length from schools are long gone and over the years we have moved well beyond the white line painted on the playground across which no parent must pass without an appointment. Now parents move freely in and out of schools and very often are found in the classrooms backing up the teachers. Both sides of the partnership know how important it is that children should be challenged and stimulated both in and out of school.

Perhaps the most vital part of this book is where parents and children are encouraged to develop activities beyond those offered on the page. The more the children explore and use the ideas and techniques we want them to learn, the more they will make new knowledge of their very own. It's not just getting the right answer, it's growing as a person through gaining skill in action and not only in books. The best way to learn is to live.

I remember reading a story to a group of nine year old boys. The story was about soldiers and of course the boys, bloodthirsty as ever, were hanging on my every word. I came to the word khaki and I asked the group "What colour is khaki?" One boy was quick to answer. "Silver," he said, "It's silver." "Silver?" I queried. "Yes," he said with absolute confidence, "Silver, my Dad's car key is silver." Now I reckon I'm a pretty good teller of stories to children but when it came down to it, all my dramatic reading of a gripping story gave way immediately to the power of the boy's experience of life. That meant so much more to him, as it does to all children.

JOHN COE
National Association for Primary Education (NAPE).

Parents and teachers work together in NAPE to improve the quality of learning and teaching in primary schools. We campaign hard for a better deal for children at the vital early stage of their education upon which later success depends. We are always pleased to hear from parents.

NAPE, Moulton College, Moulton, Northampton, NN3 7RR,
Telephone: 01604 647 646 Web: www.nape.org.uk

Writing has been devised to help you support your child in their English school work from ages 4 to 7, and will help prepare them for subsequent years.

Through a series of fun activities and questions, you will work through, together, the range of subjects that your child can expect to encounter at this age and after. Reading and writing are closely linked and the skills a child learns from reading can be transferred to their own compositions.

- Ensure your child is comfortable and alert before they sit down with the book.

- Each topic begins with an introduction, **Parents Start Here**, which will give you more information and will explain its relevance or relationship to other topics covered at this age.

- Boxes labelled **Activity** appear throughout the book. They direct the child towards other activities, to be conducted away from the book. Please read this section through with your child.

- The questions and activities in the book aim to introduce new ideas and concepts in a fun way.

- Keep a dictionary and thesaurus to hand.

- Do not attempt to complete too many pages at a time. Ten to 15 minutes is normally enough for most children at this age.

Pages of handwriting practice appear throughout the book. Let your child complete these at their own pace. It is important children do not tire while practising their handwriting or they will develop bad habits. By 7 years old, children are expected to join all their letters, except capitals – but children vary enormously in their ability to do this. Some schools teach cursive (joined) writing from nursery, while others do not allow their students to join up until aged 6 or 7.

There is a checklist at the end of the book; use this to motivate your child and help them to see how much learning they have achieved.

Most importantly, the time you spend together with this book should be enjoyable for both of you.

Parents Start Here...

Starting at 7 years old, your child will begin to learn some new spelling strategies, including the way that some words change when suffixes or prefixes are added. This activity helps your child find double consonants in words.

Doubles

a b c d e f g h i j k l m n o p q r s t u v w x y z

Coco the Clown is holding a huge balloon.

Write all the words with double consonants into the balloon:

Lollipop has double l.

careless

wet

sunny

careful

sad

wettest

sadder

sun

Join the word to its pair. One has been done for you:

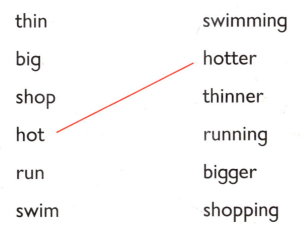

thin   swimming

big   hotter

shop   thinner

hot   running

run   bigger

swim   shopping

Did you notice that all of the words in the second list have double consonants?

Write a sentence using the word drumming:

_____

_____

Activity

The alphabet contains vowels and consonants. Write out all of the vowels and all of the consonants in two lists. Learn the vowels off by heart.

Check Your Progress!

Doubles

Turn to page 32 and put a tick next to what you have just learned.

Top Tip!
Always look for positive aspects to your child's work as well as helping them to resolve errors.

Parents Start Here...

Check your child has a sharp pencil and can hold it correctly. If your child's feet do not touch the floor when sitting, find a box they can rest their feet on. At 7 years old, children are expected to join letters. Schools have different handwriting policies, so it may be that your child doesn't join certain letters in the same way demonstrated here. However, most of it will be almost identical.

Handwriting Practice

Copy the phrases using your best handwriting. Try to join all of the letters in each word, except for capital letters.

I see you in my dreams

Blue is my favourite group

Peter always watches Newsround

Van Gogh was an artist

Daffodils grow in February

don't mention it

thank you for my present

Activity

Experiment with different pencils and pens to find one that suits your handwriting. If you press too hard, try a mechanical pencil; the lead will snap if you put too much pressure on it!

Check Your Progress!
Handwriting Practice
Turn to page 32 and put a tick next to what you have just learned.

Top Tip!
If your child struggles with anything, don't worry – let them go at their own pace.

Parents Start Here...

From 7 years old, children practise using verb tenses with increasing accuracy and can recognise whether a verb is used in the past, present or future tense.

Past, Present And Future

Complete the sentences then put the missing word into the grid to reveal a mystery word.

The missing words are all verbs and they are in the past, present or future tense.

1. Uncle Bob's carpet is filthy because he does not like to _____ it. (present)

2. I will _____ up the bin with all of this rubbish. (future)

3. The teacher _____ up the broken glass using a broom. (past)

4. Dad will _____ the car on Saturday. (future)

5. I am _____ my clothes. (present)

6. Last year Gran _____ a great Christmas dinner. (past)

7. I always _____ the ornaments first, then I put them back on the shelf. (present)

1. | V | | | | | |
2. | F | | | |
3. | S | | | | |
4. | W | | | |
5. | I | | | | |
6. | C | | | |
7. | D | | | |

The mystery word is: _____

Activity

TRY THIS

Can you make your own word puzzle like the one here? Use animal names instead of verbs, it's easier!

Check Your Progress!
Past, Present And Future
Turn to page 32 and put a tick next to what you have just learned.

Parents Start Here...

Children not only learn how to write fiction, they also learn how to present information and write clear instructions.

Instructional Texts

Here are some jumbled up instructions for making meringues. Write them out again, putting them in the right order.

Recipe: a list of cooking instructions.

Whisk the eggs on a high speed, using an electric whisk.

Put spoonfuls of the egg mixture on to a lightly greased baking tray.

Put six egg whites into a clean bowl.

When the eggs begin to go stiff add a spoonful of sugar.

Put the tray in the oven and leave the meringues for at least two hours.

Preheat the oven to 70°C.

When the egg whites make peaks do not whisk them any more.

1. _____

2. _____

3. _____

4. _____

5. _____

6. _____

7. _____

TRY THIS

Activity

If you have got the instructions in the right order you could make the meringues yourself (with an adult's help). Meringues dry out, rather than bake, so you must have the oven on a very low setting.

Check Your Progress!

Instructional Texts

Turn to page 32 and put a tick next to what you have just learned.

Top Tip!
If your child loses concentration here, let them take a break.

Parents Start Here...

As your child develops their writing they need to use more expressive language. Onomatopoeic words can add life to a piece of writing and are fun for children to use.

Words With A Sound

Onomatopoeia: when a word makes the same sound it is describing, e.g. hiss, splash, slop, woof, etc.

Join each animal to the word that describes the sound it makes:

purr

roar

cluck

bleat

neigh

moo

Circle the onomatopoeic words that you think are best:

The bacon and sausages rattled / crackled in the frying pan.

The car pinged / screeched to a halt at the red lights.

The silly boy popped / crashed the balloon with a pin.

The silver spoons clattered / whizzed to the floor.

The huge bumble bee quacked / buzzed as it flew past me.

Activity

TRY THIS

Try to use onomatopoeic words when you are telling someone a story. This will make it much more exciting for the listener.

Check Your Progress!
Words With A Sound

Turn to page 32 and put a tick next to what you have just learned.

13

Parents Start Here...

Planning stories or non-fictional accounts is an essential skill. This exercise not only helps with planning, but will help your child think about a topic laterally.

Word Webs

Vivek has sketched out a plan for the story of 'The Three Little Pigs'. Look at it carefully:

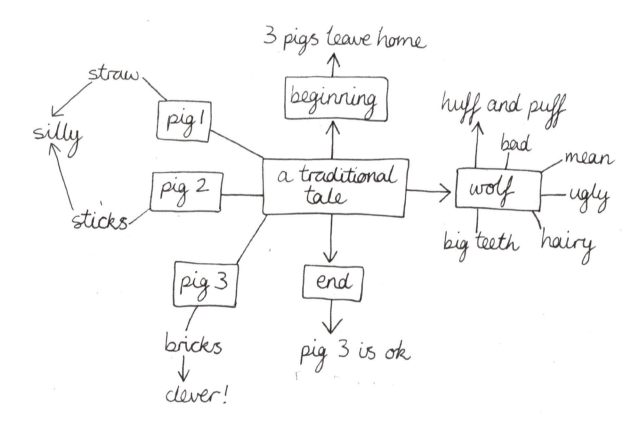

This is called a word web, or mind map. You can use word webs to plan a story.

Use the word web to answer these questions:

1. Who are the main characters in the story?

_____

2. What type of story is it?

_____

3. What did the pigs build their houses from?

_____

4. Write some words that describe the wolf:

_____

5. How did the story end?

_____

Activity

Try to draw your own word web for a fairy story, such as Cinderella. What words could you use to describe her horrid sisters?

Check Your Progress!

Word Webs

Turn to page 32 and put a tick next to what you have just learned.

15

Parents Start Here...

Your child will soon be familiar with the term prefix. Prefixes are added to root words and change them, e.g. un, il, de and dis are prefixes which often give root words the opposite meaning.

Different And The Same

Antonyms: words that mean the opposite, e.g. up/down.
Synonyms: words that mean almost the same thing.

The magnets are attracting words that mean the opposite. Draw a line between each magnet and its antonym:

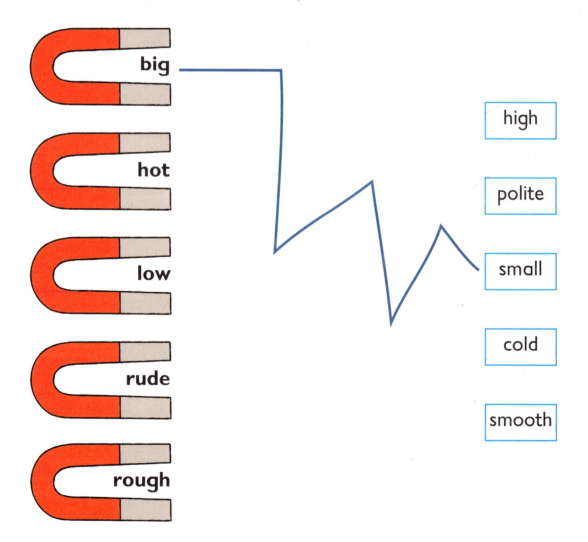

big · high · polite · small · cold · smooth

hot

low

rude

rough

Thesaurus: this is a book that contains lots of words. You can look up 'sad' and find other words that mean almost the same thing.

Use the correct synonym from this list to complete each sentence:

stop grin correct quick

Dogs can run fast but cats are _____ too.

I shouted "halt!" but the kids did not _____ in time.

Monkeys can't smile but Mum says I _____ like a chimp.

She said that 'red' is the _____ answer, but I think 'blue' was right.

 Activity

Use a thesaurus to find other ways to say 'happy'. If you find any words you really like, you can jot them down in a notebook and you'll have them to hand when you want to write a story or poem.

Check Your Progress!
Different And The Same
Turn to page 32 and put a tick next to what you have just learned.

Top Tip!
If your child struggles with anything, don't worry – let them go at their own pace.

Parents Start Here...

At this age, children are expected to understand the importance of non-fiction, as well as fiction. Signs and notices are one way that information is presented.

Silly Signs

These signs have some mistakes. Spot the mistakes, then write the signs out again properly.

BEWEAR: WILD HENS

No eggsit

Won Way

STAY ON THE WRITE

Bus Shop

No Smokeing

Activity

Write and decorate your own sign to go on your bedroom door.

Check Your Progress!

Silly Signs

Turn to page 32 and put a tick next to what you have just learned.

Top Tip! Remember to give your child lots of praise – they will work so much better.

Parents Start Here...

Research has shown that joined-up handwriting helps children remember spellings because it helps them recognise the shape and pattern each word makes.

Handwriting Practice

Copy the phrases using your best handwriting. Try to join all of the letters in each word, except for capital letters.

a boy ran in front of a car

the pig had a curly tail

sharks have sharp teeth

she's milking a cow

Dad hates shopping

I got my camping badge

Nemo is a clown fish

Tom went to the theatre

Activity

Try to write the whole alphabet, from a to z, in one joined-up word. It is pretty difficult! Keep practising until you can keep all of the letters the right size and shape.

Check Your Progress!
Handwriting Practice
Turn to page 32 and put a tick next to what you have just learned.

Top Tip!
Learning is fun, so if your child is tired, let them come back to this when they are fresh.

Parents Start Here...

Your child should be able to use full stops and capital letters appropriately, write complete sentences and use commas in a list. The use of question marks and exclamation marks will be revised around 7 years old. Speech marks will be introduced around 6 years old.

Punctuation

These are speech marks " ". They show what is being said.

Join the fisherman to the right fish.

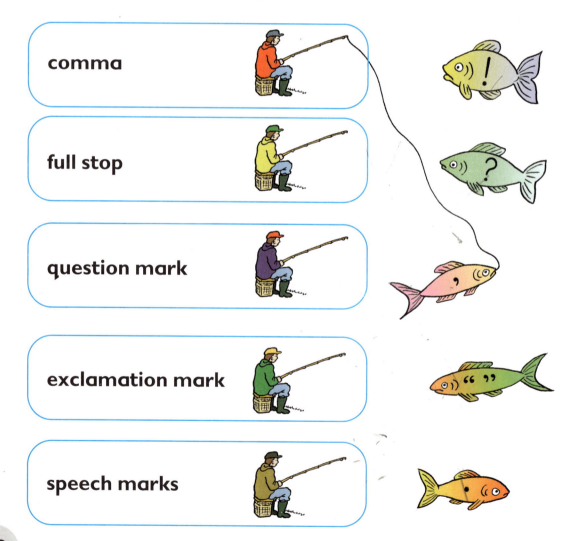

comma

full stop

question mark

exclamation mark

speech marks

The boy is speaking.

Write down what the boy is saying:

The boy says " _____ ".

The girl is speaking.

Write down what the girl is saying:

The girl says " _____ ".

Activity

Look in your story books to find speech marks. You will notice that when another person starts to speak the writing starts on a new line.

Check Your Progress!

Punctuation

Turn to page 32 and put a tick next to what you have just learned.

Top Tip! Always look for positive aspects to your child's work as well as helping them to resolve errors.

Parents Start Here...

Introduce your child to different types of poetry, including those of different cultures. Young children particularly enjoy comic verse and limericks, but your child may be ready to read some more serious poems.

Writing Rhymes

Here is a word bank. See if you can find any words that rhyme and write them in the spaces provided. Cross them off as you use them.

book	dumb	hutch	flower	poor	trouble	linger	rush
finger	grass	brush	wreck	knock	table	dew	shower
folder	track	snail	hose	phone	boulder	touch	door
look	snow	nose	deck	straw	flow	fable	laugh
queue	brass	bring	half	hail	bubble	think	bone
knack	thumb	broad	sock	paw	hoard	stink	string

nose	hose

Activity

Remember that poems don't have to rhyme and they can be a really good way to write down all your feelings. Try writing a poem about something, or someone, you feel very strongly about. It might be something you like or really don't like.

Check Your Progress!
Writing Rhymes ☐
Turn to page 32 and put a tick next to what you have just learned.

25

Parents Start Here...

At 7 years old, children extend their knowledge of plurals. They should understand the term 'collective noun' and recognise that some nouns, such as trousers, cannot be pluralised.

One Or More

A noun that tells us that there is just one of something is called a singular noun, e.g. egg.

A noun that tells us that there is more than one of something is called a plural noun, e.g. eggs.

A noun is a naming word.

Add s to each word to turn it into a plural:

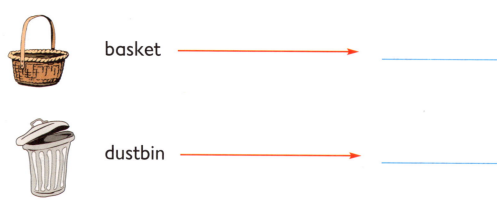

basket ⟶ _____

dustbin ⟶ _____

tub ⟶ _____

Nouns that end in f usually change the f to v, then add es e.g. loaf ⟶ loaves.

Complete the table:

Single	Plural
knife	
	thieves
calf	
	wives

Nouns that end in ch, x, sh or s (remember them as 'snake noises') also add es in the plural.

Complete the table:

Single	Plural
church	
	boxes
dish	
	buses

Some nouns have unusual plurals. Write the singular of each word below its picture:

mice children men geese

_____ _____ _____ _____

Activity

Find out the plurals of things around your home. You need to learn the spellings of the plurals off by heart, so get practising!

Check Your Progress!

One Or More

Turn to page 32 and put a tick next to what you have just learned.

Top Tip!
Go through any of the questions on these pages as often as you like until your child understands it fully.

Parents Start Here...

When children learn to do joined-up writing, the letters sometimes get smaller. This is fine, as long as the writing is still legible and neat, and the letters stay in proportion.

Handwriting Practice

Copy the phrases using your best handwriting. Try to join all of the letters in each word:

sing a song for me

hit the drum

I love cherry tomatoes

no more chips please

monkeys are funny

the little hand was on two

the hen sat on her egg

the bus is always late

Activity

Practise writing words just using capital letters. You might use capital letters to write signs, posters and leaflets.

Check Your Progress!

Handwriting Practice

Turn to page 32 and put a tick next to what you have just learned.

Answers

Pages 4–5

Words with double consonants:
careless, sunny, wettest, sadder.

thin	thinner
big	bigger
shop	shopping
run	running
swim	swimming

Pages 8–9

1. vacuum
2. fill
3. swept
4. wash
5. ironing
6. cooked
7. dust

The mystery word is 'cleaned'.

Pages 10–11

1. Preheat the oven to 70°C.
2. Put six egg whites into a clean bowl.
3. Whisk the eggs on a high speed, using an electric whisk.
4. When the eggs begin to go stiff add a spoonful of sugar.
5. When the egg whites make peaks do not whisk them any more.
6. Put spoonfuls of the egg mixture on to a lightly greased baking tray.
7. Put the tray in the oven and leave the meringues for at least two hours.

Pages 12–13

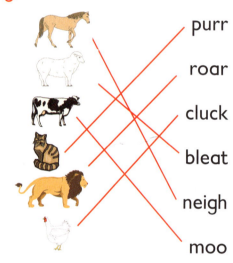

purr

roar

cluck

bleat

neigh

moo

Crackled, screeched, popped, clattered, buzzed.

Pages 14–15

Main characters: Wolf, pig 1, pig 2 and pig 3.
The story is a traditional tale.
The pigs built their houses from straw, sticks and bricks.
The wolf is bad, mean, ugly, hairy, has big teeth and huffs and puffs.
Pig 3 is okay at the end.

Pages 16–17
hot/cold
low/high
rude/polite
rough/smooth
Dogs can run fast but cats are quick too.
I shouted "halt!" but the kids did not stop in time.
Monkeys can't smile but Mum says I grin like a chimp.
She said that 'red' is the correct answer, but I think 'blue' was right.

Pages 18–19
BEWARE: WILD HENS
No Exit
One Way
STAY ON THE RIGHT
Bus Stop
No Smoking

Pages 22–23
Comma: ,
Full stop: .
Question mark: ?
Exclamation mark: !
Speech marks " "
The boy says "I am hungry".
The girl says "I like cats".

Pages 24–25
book / look   finger / linger
folder / boulder   queue / dew
knack / track   dumb / thumb

grass / brass   snow / flow
hutch / touch   brush / rush
snail / hail   bring / string
broad / hoard   flower / shower
wreck / deck   half / laugh
sock / knock   phone / bone
trouble / bubble   table / fable
think / stink   nose / hose
poor / straw / door / paw

Pages 26–27
Plurals: baskets, dustbins, tubs.

Single	Plural
knife	knives
thief	thieves
calf	calves
wife	wives

Single	Plural
church	churches
box	boxes
dish	dishes
bus	buses

 goose

 man

 mouse

 child

31

Check Your Progress!

Doubles.. ☑

Handwriting Practice .... ☑

Past, Present And Future .... ☑

Instructional Texts .... ☐

Words With A Sound .... ☐

Word Webs .... ☐

Different And The Same........................ ☐

Silly Signs .... ☐

Handwriting Practice .... ☐

Punctuation .... ☐

Writing Rhymes................................. ☐

One Or More .... ☐

Handwriting Practice .... ☐